Commissioned by the Tucson Music Teachers Association for their 60th Anniversary Piano Ensemble Concert. March 2013

Tucson Toccata

AF817355

PRIMO

Fast and bubbling over (𝅗𝅥 = ca. 104)

Robert D. Vandall

SECONDO

PRIMO

SECONDO

PRIMO

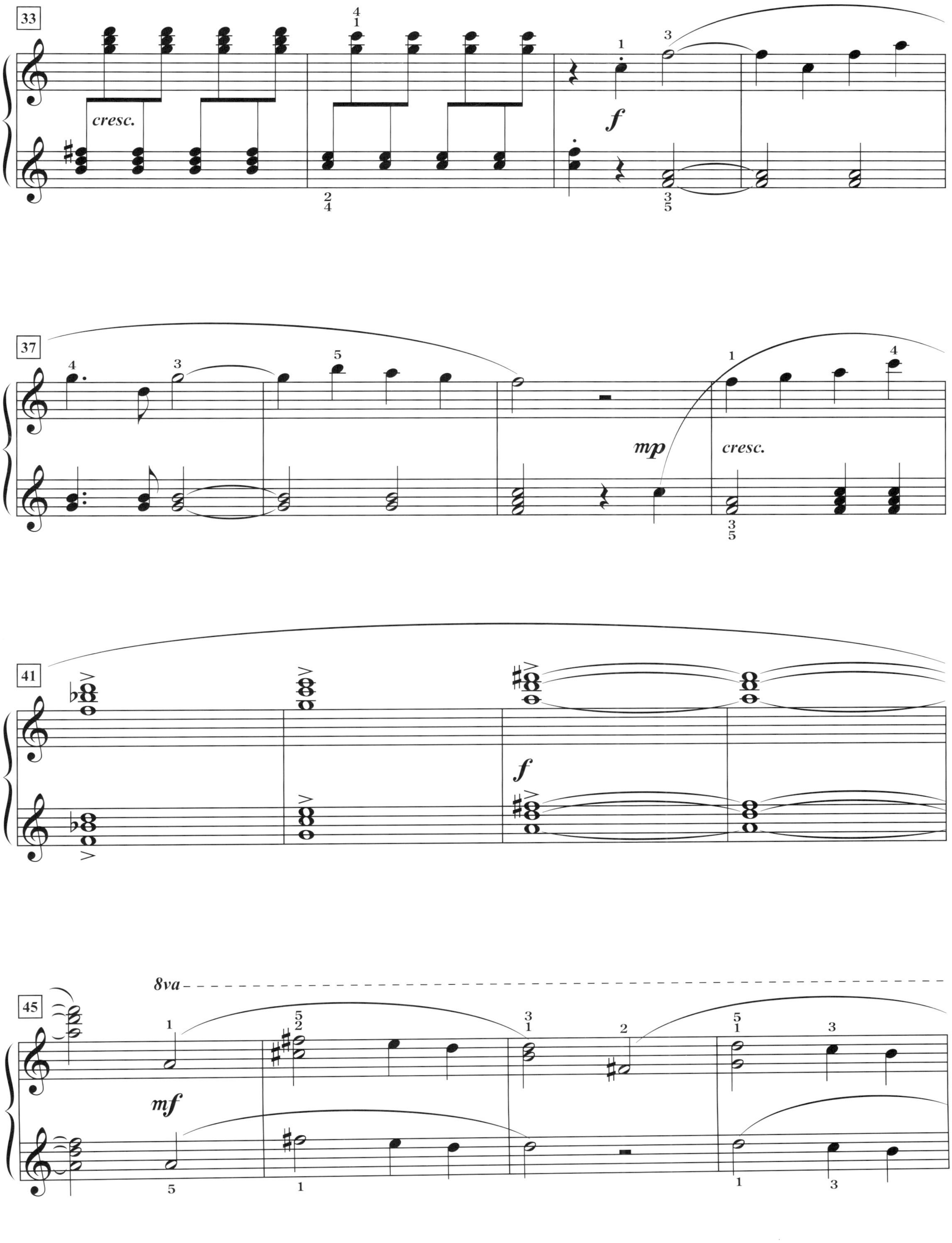

SECONDO

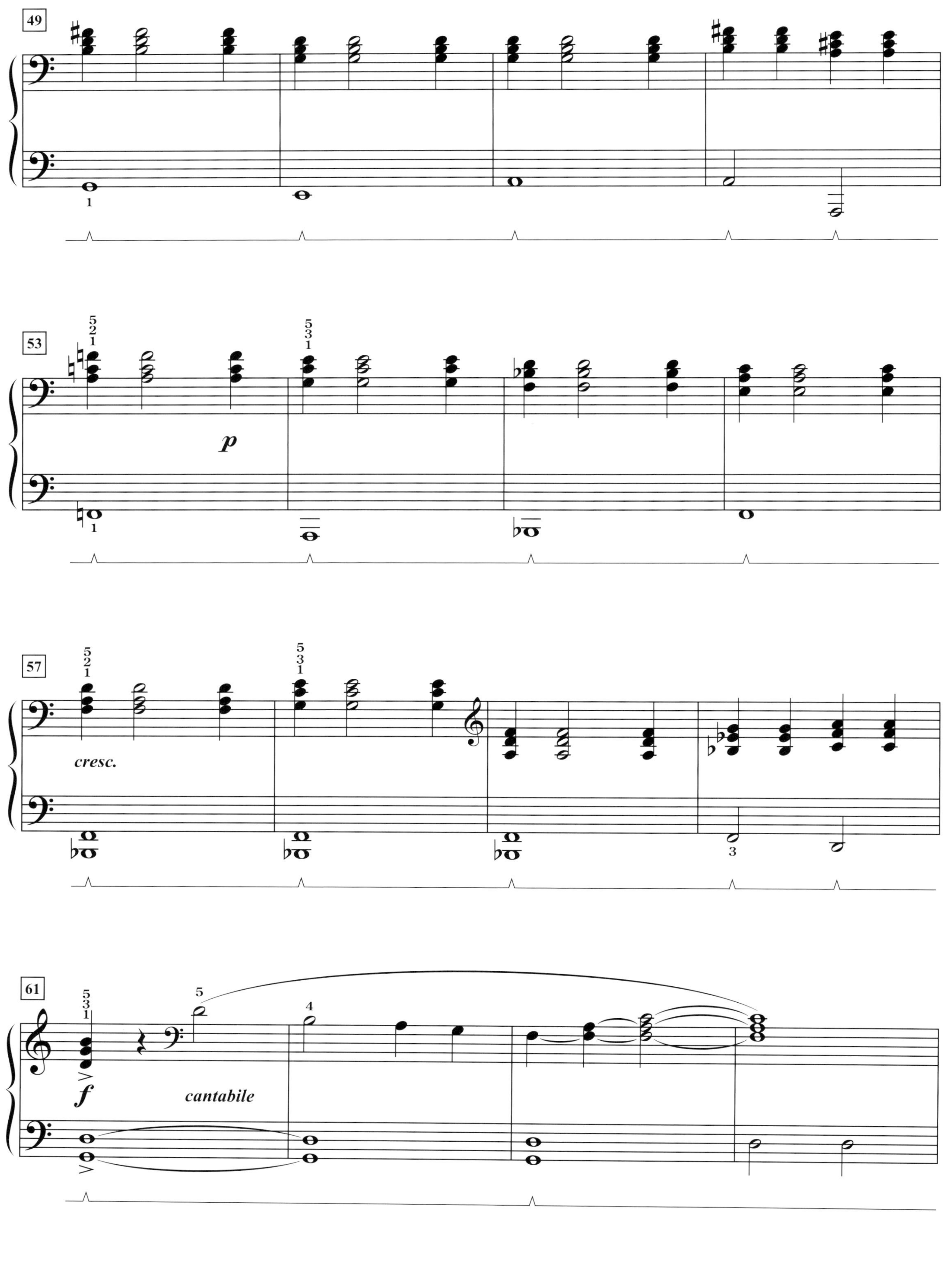

PRIMO

65
69
mf
73
cresc.
77
f
mf

65
69
8va
p
73
cresc.
77
f

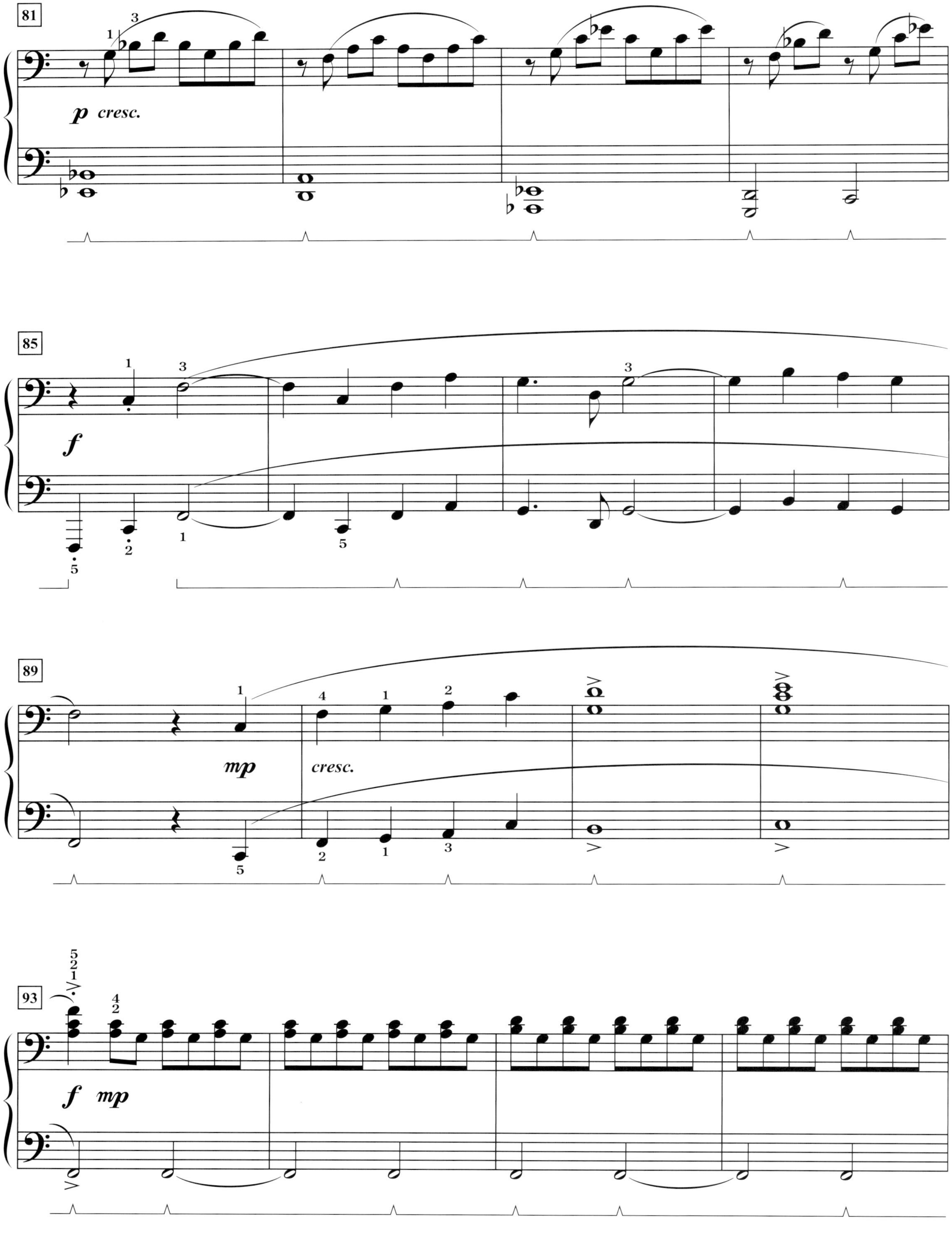
81
p cresc.
85
f
89
mp
cresc.
93
f mp

81
mp cresc.
85
f mp
89
p
cresc.
93
f

SECONDO